VIRTUE STORIES

What a Team!

Lalita Iyer

**Om
KIDZ**
An imprint of Om Books International

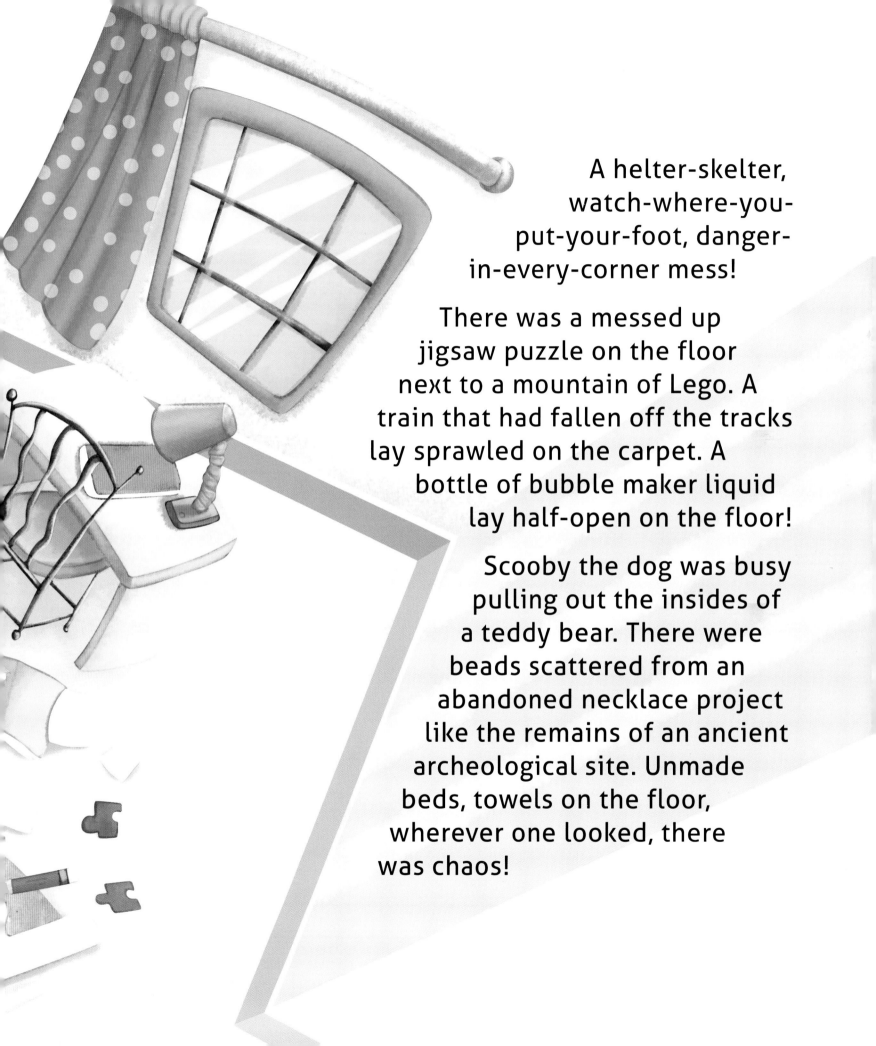

A helter-skelter, watch-where-you-put-your-foot, danger-in-every-corner mess!

There was a messed up jigsaw puzzle on the floor next to a mountain of Lego. A train that had fallen off the tracks lay sprawled on the carpet. A bottle of bubble maker liquid lay half-open on the floor!

Scooby the dog was busy pulling out the insides of a teddy bear. There were beads scattered from an abandoned necklace project like the remains of an ancient archeological site. Unmade beds, towels on the floor, wherever one looked, there was chaos!

Mama entered, looked around and lost it. 'Kids, I'm telling you for the last time,' accidently stepping on a Lego piece.

'Ouch!' She screamed. 'I have had enough of this mess!'

Just then, a magna tiles house that Anya had built for her dolls, collapsed. The house was taller than she, so, naturally, it had to.'Why don't you put the toys you don't need in your toy closet?' Mama said, trying to open the cupboard.

'DON'T!' Pat and Anya screamed. It was too late.

Mama was now buried under a pile of stuffed dolls, board games, more Lego, a doll house, several balls, toy cars and hula hoops.

'Enough is enough!' She screamed. Pin drop silence.

'I am tired of always picking up after you kids and straightening your room. If you are not going to have it spick and span in two days, I am donating all your toys and things to the thrift store. And that is that!'

She walked off in a huff. Pat, Anya and Scooby looked at each other. When Mama said, 'That is that!' it was always serious.

The room was seriously, a mess. That night at dinner, Mama was very quiet as she passed the food around. Papa was quiet too. The kids knew it was serious!

The next morning, there was a knock.

It was Papa. 'Kids, let's do this together. We are a team. Let's divide and conquer.'

Pat and Anya were excited; Scooby was, too. 'Where do we start, Papa?' Pat said, trying to figure out the beginning of the mess.

'Boxes,' said Papa. 'First, we need boxes.'

For the next two hours, Pat and Anya went about the house, collecting as many boxes as they could. They picked boxes from the basement, from the garage, and even from the study.

They now had quite a few. 'Now we need to label them and sort things into them.'

So they began labelling.

Anya had good handwriting, so she took over. Pat began the sorting.

Games. Rocks. Clay. Shells. Feathers. Pencils. Crayons. Glue. String. Model kits. Lego. Magna tiles. Puzzles. Blocks. Dolls. Doll clothes. Cards. Balls.

Gosh, they had a lot of stuff!

When they were all in boxes, it didn't look like a lot.

Even Scooby helped! He was incharge of the ball box.

And there was still some stuff that didn't belong anywhere.

'Wait!' Papa said. 'Are you willing to give this away?'

'YES!' They said.

So Papa got another box and wrote 'TO GIVE AWAY' on it.

'Next, we need to sweep this mess,' he said.

Anya, who always imagined she would fly away on a magic broom, grabbed one. 'I'll do this.'

Pat made the beds.

Just then, Mama walked in. 'What have you guys been upto? Haven't seen you all day.'

She looked at the room and couldn't believe her eyes!

'This is great work! How did you manage all this in just a day?'

Pat pointed to Anya and
Anya pointed to Scooby
and Scooby ran up to Papa
and started wagging his
tail real hard!

'It was all team work!' Papa said. 'Each one of us did something.' 'And a lot felt like a little,' said Pat and Anya.

'What a team!' said Mama, joyfully. 'The best ever!' She said, giving everyone a group hug.

Never give Up

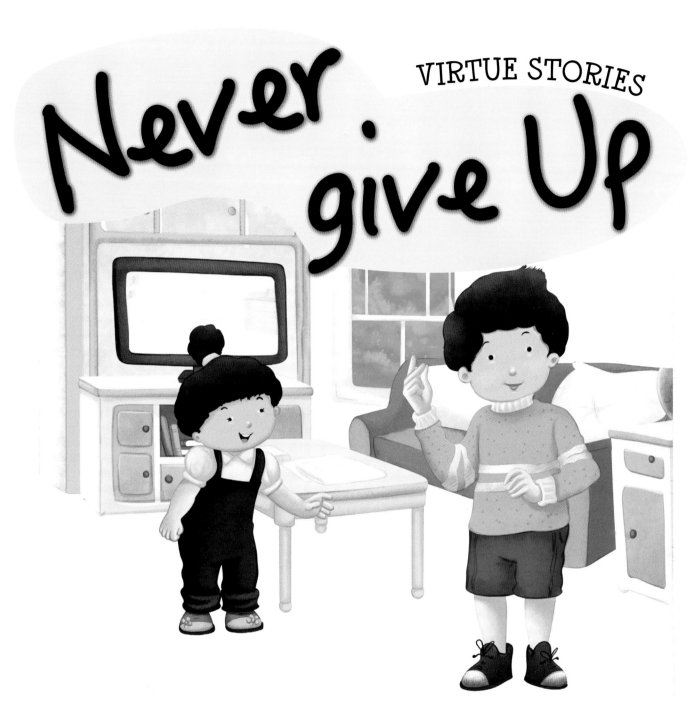

Lalita Iyer

Om KIDZ

An imprint of Om Books International

Ishaan watched his three-year-old sister carefully. *There! She's done it again,* he thought.

He pressed his thumbs against his middle fingers, took a moment, and then brushed them against each other. No click.

He tried again. And again.

But his fingers refused to click in that nice 'click-click-click' manner that he was so keen to master.

His sister Ina was lolling on the bean bag and watching TV, but he knew she was watching him really, so he ignored her.

'Like this,' she said and clicked her fingers loudly.

He turned his back to her. Ina was so annoying.

Sometimes, she would start winking with both eyes alternately - he never knew how she did it! That was even more annoying.

Such a show off, he thought. *But I am going to keep trying till I get it...*

He held his hands in his lap and practised the clicks. His fingers softly and silently brushed past each other. He decided to give it a break and pressed his hands together, giving them a gentle massage.

'Like this,' Ina called out. This time he looked over. She held up her hands, pressed her thumb against her middle fingers and released! Click!

Ishaan held up his right hand. He pressed his thumb against his middle finger. He took a deep breath.

The fingers passed by each other in total silence. Ina winked at him, first with her left eye, then with her right. 'Don't give up,' she chuckled, and turned back to watch TV. Ishaan did the only thing he could do. He stuck his tongue out at her!

Bored, he picked up the two ping-pong balls on the table and randomly started throwing them in the air. He soon realised he could throw both up and pick them up at the same time. *Let me try something else*, he thought. Ina was now watching him very closely.

Ishaan now tried again, hoping it wouldn't slip. It didn't. Balls up in the air, Ishaan's eyes were shifting from one ball to the next, as one went up and the other went down. And he kept on, and on, and on at it.

Next he threw one ball a second after the other, and soon caught them in the opposite hand. Ina clapped when it happened. 'Hey, that's called juggling! I want to learn too!'

Ina was clapping loudly, cheering her big brother on, who was now officially, her favourite juggler!

VIRTUE STORIES
Play Fair

Lalita Iyer

An imprint of Om Books International

Sharon hopped and skipped to the play area with her brand-new ball. As she entered, she noticed a group of kids. As soon as they saw her, they moved away.

'No one wants to play with me,' she wailed. 'No one wants to be my friend.'

Her brother Aron who was jumping on the trampoline, noticed her whining. 'Maybe because you don't play fair?' he said.

'What do you mean?' she asked.

'You are five. You should know,' he said, like a grown up. Sharon hated it when Aron acted all grown up although he was just three years older to her.

'Okay, come jump with me on the trampoline and I will explain,' he said. Each time you answer, you have to jump higher, okay?'

'Okay.'

'So, what do you do when you lose in a game?'

Sharon knew the answer and she was embarrassed. 'I cry,' she said and jumped.

'Is that all?'

'No wait, I insist on winning,' she said,
and jumped higher.
'I also feel sad when I lose. I hate losing.'

Aron rolled his eyes.

'Hmm, so what do you do when someone takes your teddy to play with it? '

'Well, I …. I scream and shout till she gives it back to me.' But her lips were quivering as she said it.

'You forgot to jump,' said Aron.

'Oh, yes.'

'Why does it make you mad when someone takes your things?'

'Because they are mine.
How dare they?' Even as she
said it, she felt horrible.

'What do you do when Manu comes
home and Mama asks you to give
him a turn at the computer when
you are playing a game?'

'I get mad... but I do it sulkily
because Mama said so,' she said.

'You forgot to jump.'

When Sharon jumped this time, something changed inside her. Another Sharon within her was saying, *you know, he is right!*

Soon it was time to go home. She could hear her mother call, 'Sharon, Aron, come home. Bath time.'

As they ran inside, Sharon said, 'I am going second.'

Aron said, 'No, you go first.'

'Why?' she asked.

'Because you are younger than me,' he laughed.

'Not fair,' said Sharon and they both laughed.

VIRTUE STORIES

How Kind!

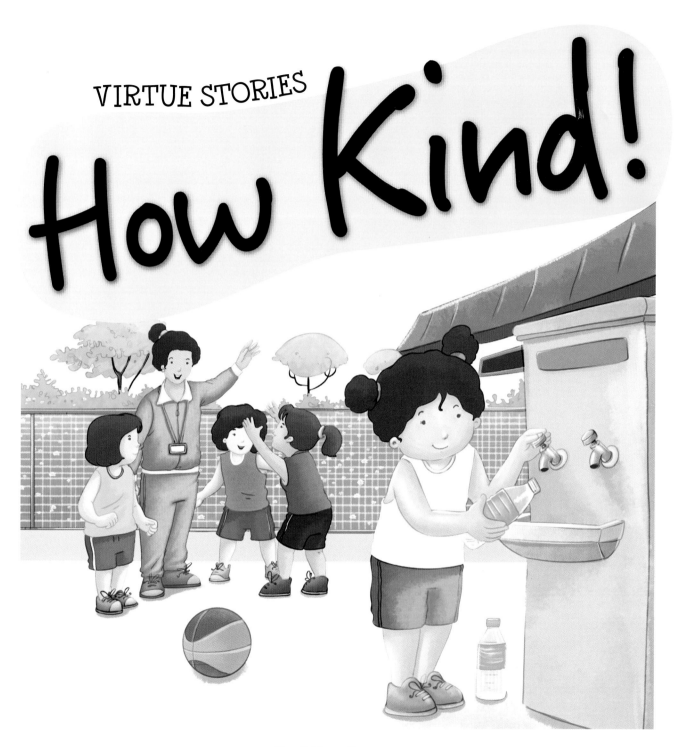

Lalita Iyer

An imprint of Om Books International

Katie put her hand up. She badly wanted to make it to the basketball team!

She adored basketball, running around the field, bouncing the ball and the moment when the ball sailed through the air and into the hoop. The last moments were rare though, as she hardly ever scored. But that never stopped her from trying.

The coach picked Sue, Anya and Tina.

She knew the coach would also go to the other sections to select girls from there. She would not pick more than four girls from Katie's class.

'Katie,' the coach called out, noting down her name and Katie pumped the air in relief. They were to meet for practice every alternate day after school. There was a match in three weeks and they must be ready!

Katie did not miss a single practice. She ran her fastest, bounced the ball as best as she could and practiced throwing the ball into the hoop again and again. She became faster, but she still wasn't scoring enough baskets as she had hoped. She was disappointed but not surprised, when she was announced as one of the substitutes.

Anya was made the captain, which was again no surprise as she was the strongest player. Sue and Tina were selected to play as well and Tina whispered to her not to be disappointed. She was sure she would get a chance.

Katie never did get a chance. She sat out every game there was, as the team moved from win to win till at last, they were through to the finals. Katie had decided after the first match that even if she didn't play at all, she would be the best cheerleader, water carrier and helper possible to the team!

They needed it and she kept her word to herself.

The team had never made it to the finals and everyone was very excited and nervous. As their coach called out the names of the players, Katie checked all the water bottles to make sure they were full. 'Katie,' she heard the coach call out.

'I'm filling the bottles, Coach,' she called back. 'Then I'll check the medical box.

'No, I'm not calling you for that. I'm calling you because you're part of the playing team. Come here and kit up.'

Katie froze. She looked at the other girls on the team and each and every one of them gave her a big grin and nodded - they all wanted her to play or they wouldn't play at all.

Katie felt like crying. Instead, she rushed over, hugged her coach, gave the girls a big thumbs up and went to pull her special shoes on.

The game was a close one and Katie didn't score a single basket, but they won in the end! Coach called Katie over and said, 'You know, Katie, you have no idea what you did for the team! Everyone felt so loved and cared for. That's what team morale is all about .... and you are great at building it.....''

Holding the cup with the coach and the team, Katie was overjoyed!

Wait for your Turn

VIRTUE STORIES

Lalita Iyer

An imprint of Om Books International

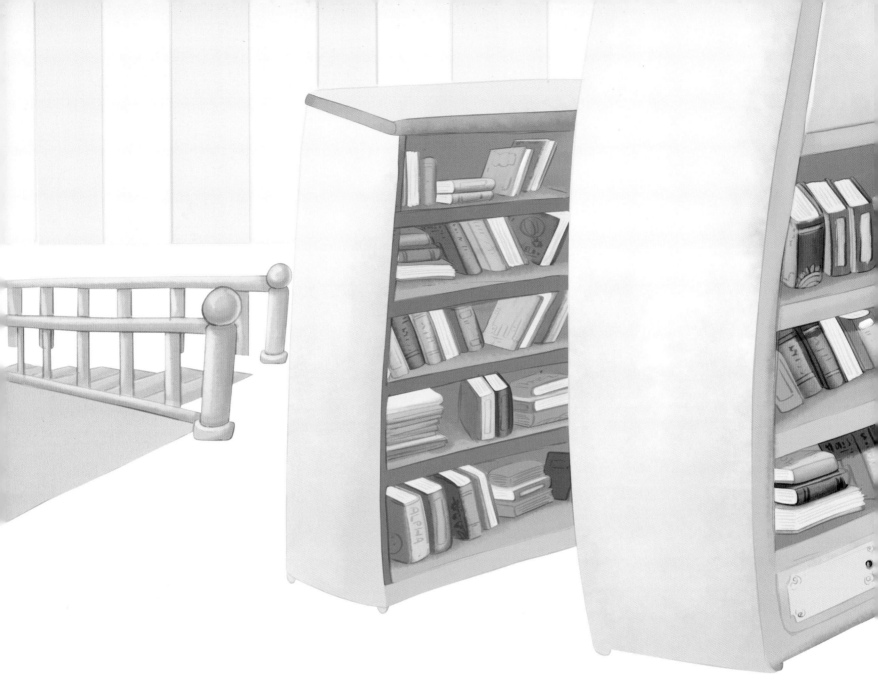

Mimi's most favourite place in the world was the good, old library in the centre of the town. Her mother took her there every weekend. She loved to spend hours crossing the ancient corridors, browsing through piles of books. Even the book lending system was old-style! She could browse and read as much as she liked, but she could only take four books home. For Mimi, this was always a difficult decision.

Mimi was lost in the wonders of ancient Egypt in a book of illustrated pictures, when her mother tapped her on the shoulder. It was time to go home.

Mimi did an eeny-meeny-mynah-moh and picked up four books from the pile she had kept aside to borrow. Just when she was about to reach the counter, a little boy, who seemed to be in a great hurry, ran past her and got there before she did.

The kind lady behind the counter, Mrs Richards, saw Mimi coming towards her first and requested the boy to wait. But since he was in a hurry to pull his books out, he didn't even see her hand gesture and as he pulled *Cursed Child* out, his pencil case spilled out too, as he had forgotten to zip it. Everything fell on the floor – including his origami birds, some paper balls, lots of coins, his football erasers and god knows what else!

By this time, three other children were in the queue and Mimi was the first. The boy got up, picked his things and looked at her apologetically. She smiled. 'It's okay, you may go first,' she said.

Mrs Richards entered the book codes and stamped them with the due date for return. She then handed the books back to the boy. He hurriedly tried stuffing them all into his small bag. They kept spilling out and he was getting more and more delayed.

Mimi waited patiently for him to leave. She, then, cheerfully went up to the counter and handed her books to Mrs Richards. The strict lady looked through her glasses, took her books, punched the numbers in and asked Mimi if she would like to come in to her side of the counter. Mimi was pleasantly surprised and excited at this. She couldn't believe her luck!

The little boy stopped what he was doing, stood up, and with his mouth open, saw what Mimi was going to be doing. *If only I had waited my turn, I too might have got to do this*, he thought.

Once Mrs Richards let Mimi in through her little side gate to her side of the counter, she handed Mimi the date stamp. She then got her to check today's date, helped her add 10 days to it and asked her to turn the stamp rails one by one and punch it on the books.

Mimi was grinning from ear to ear and was clearly having a lot of fun and feeling all important.

Once done, Mimi picked up her books and thanked Mrs Richards for having let her do the stamping. Mrs Richards in return, thanked Mimi and welcomed her to come again.

As she walked away with her mother, Mimi shared her wonder. 'Mom, who would have thought I would be able to live my dream of being a librarian today, just like the stylish Mrs Richards!' Her mother looked at her lovingly and hugged her. 'Mimi, this was the reward you got for being polite and kind in waiting patiently for your turn!'

VIRTUE STORIES

Let's shake Hands

Lalita Iyer

Om
KIDZ
An imprint of Om Books International

Antony was never going to play with Krish again. He was so mad at him!

Every time they went cycling around the block, Krish liked to bump into Antony's cycle with his own. Last evening, it made Antony fall and he had scraped his knee badly.

'Enough of cycling. I am going to play table tennis instead,' Antony muttered to himself. He was still very mad!

The next evening, Krish called out to him as he walked across to the table tennis table. Antony pretended not to hear. Krish cycled towards the table tennis table and waited for a chance as Antony played with another boy.

Antony won the game and seemed excited. Krish asked him, "Hey, can I play a game with you now?".

But Antony said he was bored and moved on to the jungle gym. Krish ran after him and asked if they could play "Swing-Like-A-Jungle-Monkey" on the bars but Antony said he hated that game.

Krish was hurt and said nothing. He stood watching Antony swing on the bars.

Antony's mother, who was taking his baby sister for a walk in her pram, called him over. She had noticed Anthony was ill- tempered that day though he would not admit it. He was irritable. She asked him the reason for his behaviour.

'Because he always bumps my cycle hard with his cycle. I don't like it. So I don't want to play with him,' Antony muttered angrily.

His mother asked if Krish played nicely with him at other times. Antony thought for a moment. Then he said, 'yes.'

His mother said that perhaps Krish did not know that Antony did not like being bumped with his cycle.

'Why don't you tell him what you like and what you don't like? Maybe, you can still have fun playing together?'

'This way you can still be friends and agree to disagree nicely so both of you don't feel sad and grumpy either.' Antony's mom reasoned with him.

Antony thought about it for a few seconds earnestly. He then walked over to where Krish was hanging from one of the jungle gym bars, a sad look on his face.

'Don't bump my cycle with yours.
I don't like it.' Antony said.

'Oh, ok, I didn't know,' said Krish. Antony stuck out his hand. Krish shook it.

A smile decorated their happy faces as they both played 'Swing-Like-A-Jungle-Monkey' for a while and later, cycled together.

This time, Krish was careful that he did not bump into Antony's cycle. Both decided that they would shake hands on anything they didn't like about each other in the future. They were good friends again!